This Journal
BELONGS TO

_____
_____

Dedication

This Pantry Inventory Journal is dedicated to all the people out there who love to track their pantry supplies and document their findings in the process.

You are my inspiration for producing books and I'm honored to be a part of keeping all of your Pantry notes, and records organized.

This journal notebook will help you record your details about tracking your pantry inventory.

Thoughtfully put together with these sections to record: Item Name, Quantity, Expiration Date, and Grocery Shopping Lists.

How to Use this Book

The purpose of this book is to keep all of your Pantry, Refrigerator, and Freezer notes all in one place. It will help keep you organized.

This Pantry Inventory Book will allow you to accurately document every detail about all of your kitchen stock including pantry, refrigerator, and freezer. It's a great way to chart your course through maintaining a well-organized kitchen.

Here are examples of the prompts for you to fill in and write about your experience in this book:

1. Item Name

2. Quantity

3. Expiration Date

4. Grocery Shopping List

Family Pantry Inventory List

Item	Quantity	Expiration Date

Family Freezer Inventory List

Item	Quantity	Date

Family Refrigerator Inventory

Item	Quantity	Expiration Date

SHOPPING LIST

Date

Family Pantry Inventory List

Item	Quantity	Expiration Date

Family Freezer Inventory List

Item	Quantity	Date

Family Refrigerator Inventory

Item	Quantity	Expiration Date

SHOPPING LIST

Date

Family Pantry Inventory List

Item	Quantity	Expiration Date

Family Freezer Inventory List

Item	Quantity	Date

Family Refrigerator Inventory

Item	Quantity	Expiration Date

SHOPPING LIST

Date

Family Pantry Inventory List

Item	Quantity	Expiration Date

Family Freezer Inventory List

Item	Quantity	Date

Family Refrigerator Inventory

Item	Quantity	Expiration Date

Shopping List

Date:

Family Pantry Inventory List

Item	Quantity	Expiration Date

Family Freezer Inventory List

Item	Quantity	Date

Family Refrigerator Inventory

Item	Quantity	Expiration Date

SHOPPING LIST

Date

Family Pantry Inventory List

Item	Quantity	Expiration Date

Family Freezer Inventory List

Item	Quantity	Date

Family Refrigerator Inventory

Item	Quantity	Expiration Date

SHOPPING LIST

Date

Family Pantry Inventory List

Item	Quantity	Expiration Date

Family Freezer Inventory List

Item	Quantity	Date

Family Refrigerator Inventory

Item	Quantity	Expiration Date

SHOPPING LIST

Date

Family Pantry Inventory List

Item	Quantity	Expiration Date

Family Freezer Inventory List

Item	Quantity	Date

Family Refrigerator Inventory

Item	Quantity	Expiration Date

SHOPPING LIST

Date

Family Pantry Inventory List

Item	Quantity	Expiration Date

Family Freezer Inventory List

Item	Quantity	Date

Family Refrigerator Inventory

Item	Quantity	Expiration Date

Shopping List

Date

Family Pantry Inventory List

Item	Quantity	Expiration Date

Family Freezer Inventory List

Item	Quantity	Date

Family Refrigerator Inventory

Item	Quantity	Expiration Date

SHOPPING LIST

Date

Family Pantry Inventory List

Item	Quantity	Expiration Date

Family Freezer Inventory List

Item	Quantity	Date

Family Refrigerator Inventory

Item	Quantity	Expiration Date

Shopping List

Date:

Family Pantry Inventory List

Item	Quantity	Expiration Date

Family Freezer Inventory List

Item	Quantity	Date

Family Refrigerator Inventory

Item	Quantity	Expiration Date

SHOPPING LIST

Date

Family Pantry Inventory List

Item	Quantity	Expiration Date

Family Freezer Inventory List

Item	Quantity	Date

Family Refrigerator Inventory

Item	Quantity	Expiration Date

SHOPPING LIST

Date

Family Pantry Inventory List

Item	Quantity	Expiration Date

Family Freezer Inventory List

Item	Quantity	Date

Family Refrigerator Inventory

Item	Quantity	Expiration Date

SHOPPING LIST

Date

Family Pantry Inventory List

Item	Quantity	Expiration Date

Family Freezer Inventory List

Item	Quantity	Date

Family Refrigerator Inventory

Item	Quantity	Expiration Date

SHOPPING LIST

Date

Family Pantry Inventory List

Item	Quantity	Expiration Date

Family Freezer Inventory List

Item	Quantity	Date

Family Refrigerator Inventory

Item	Quantity	Expiration Date

SHOPPING LIST

Date

Family Pantry Inventory List

Item	Quantity	Expiration Date

Family Freezer Inventory List

Item	Quantity	Date

Family Refrigerator Inventory

Item	Quantity	Expiration Date

Shopping List

Date

Family Pantry Inventory List

Item	Quantity	Expiration Date

Family Freezer Inventory List

Item	Quantity	Date

Family Refrigerator Inventory

Item	Quantity	Expiration Date

Shopping List

Date

Family Pantry Inventory List

Item	Quantity	Expiration Date

Family Freezer Inventory List

Item	Quantity	Date

Family Refrigerator Inventory

Item	Quantity	Expiration Date

Shopping List

Date

Family Pantry Inventory List

Item	Quantity	Expiration Date

Family Freezer Inventory List

Item	Quantity	Date

Family Refrigerator Inventory

Item	Quantity	Expiration Date

SHOPPING LIST

Date

www.ingramcontent.com/pod-product-compliance
Lightning Source LLC
Chambersburg PA
CBHW071317080526
44587CB00018B/3256